JJ Waller's
Brighton
Vol:02

Introduction
Mark Power, Magnum Photos

'Familiarity', as we know, 'breeds contempt'. But to many photographers familiarity breeds something quite different: a kind of blindness. In the everyday, in the familiar, it can be difficult to *really* see anything at all.

That's why, throughout the checkered history of the medium, we photographers have traditionally gone in search of the exotic, boarding a plane to a distant country, or turning our cameras on people from a different social class. I'm afraid I've been guilty of both.

I moved to Brighton in 1978 to attend art school and I'm still here, yet I've rarely photographed my adopted city. With each passing year I regret my laziness (for that is what it is) more and more, yet I never seem to do anything about it. It's too easy to convince myself I'll do it tomorrow, or next month, or even next year. But places change, and Brighton probably faster than most; a walk through the North Laines never fails to surprise as we notice yet another new business on the site of one that failed.

But Brighton, I too easily tell myself, is already over-photographed, so why add more? Take a trip down to the seafront, particularly at weekends, and you'll find stag and hen parties armed to the teeth with iPhones (and other models that are available...) manically documenting everything they do. But then again, what happens to those pictures? The best might reach Facebook or a similar social media page, but that's probably it. So perhaps there is a point, after all?

As I write this I'm reminded of some of the photographic greats who have been attracted to Brighton: Walker Evans, Diane Arbus, Henri Cartier-Bresson, Roger Mayne, Felix Mann, Daniel Meadows, Martin Parr and many others. Certain subjects reoccur: there was a Mr Phillips who, in his later years, would regularly paddle in the same spot, trousers rolled up to his knees, cloth cap pulled down tightly over his head, just to the east of the Palace Pier. Over a decade he was photographed by Tony Ray Jones, Elliott Erwitt, and Lord Snowdon. Few could claim they've modeled for such an illustrious band.

And then there's JJ Waller, brought up in Brighton. A glance at his CV tells us he's 'been around' and although a serious interest in photography arrived a little later, when it came it was informed with a deep understanding of the theatre of the street. To continue this analogy, the American Joel Meyerowitz once likened street photography to watching a stage, huge waves throwing up one actor after another in an ever-changing play impossible to predict, control or direct. OK, he was mixing his metaphors a bit, and he was talking specifically about New York, but he has a point: wait for long enough on the streets of Brighton and something extraordinary will happen.

And so, in the fine tradition of the street photographer, JJ Waller prowls the pavements day in, day out, in search of the unexpected. The beauty of

His pictures benefit from repeated viewings because of the layers of information in each picture.

working like this is that you can never predict what you'll find; everyday is a potential adventure. However, let's not underestimate the time and commitment required to reap the benefits. Skimming through this book a casual reader might think it's easy to make pictures in a place like Brighton, which has traditionally attracted the... um... unusual. But, believe me, there'll be many wasted hours and days when things don't quite turn out as planned. That said, large-scale, preplanned events – Gay Pride, the naked bike ride, the vintage car rally and all the other strange and wonderful gatherings that grace our city almost every weekend - are likely to throw up excellent photo opportunities, but it's difficult to avoid cliché. Certainly, Waller revels in these events (the exotic, if you like) but he doesn't confine himself to

them. In fact, many of the best pictures in this book are of nothing much at all... they are just well seen.

No matter how bizarre a situation he might come across Waller still has to make a photograph of it; it's not just a matter of plonking the point of interest in the centre and pushing the button. The picture must 'work', or it won't last; we'd simply get the joke and move on. Thankfully though, his pictures benefit from repeated viewings because of the layers of information in each picture, and the often unfortunate clashes therein. A group of women, for instance, wait at a bus stop, blissfully ignorant of the slightly excited and frankly rather alarming naked man lurking behind the hedge.

Picture after picture provokes a chuckle. Who would have thought the

rebuilding of the Seven Dials roundabout could make such a witty picture, so neat and tidy but for the single anarchic orange bollard that's fallen out of line? The sequencing is good too: in some of the more successful pairings Waller plays with our perception, one picture bouncing off another until we start to see something else emerge between the two. The man in the heavy black overcoat, for instance, staring out to sea through a blanket of snow, takes on the characteristics of an enormous bird, an evil crow perhaps, while a wooden fence morphs effortlessly into metal.

So thank you Mr Waller for making these pictures, for making me smile, and for making me get off my backside and take my camera for a walk.

Mark Power, Brighton, October 2014

SORRY!
WE DONT D
SKINNY OR FATTY LATTES
MOCHA CHOCA
COFFEE WITH SPRINKLES
AND SYRUP
OR CAPPUCINO WITH
EXTRA FROTH AND
CHOC DUSTING + GOLD
SPARKLES
WE ONLY DO INSTANT
GOLD BLEND yum yum in your
tum tum

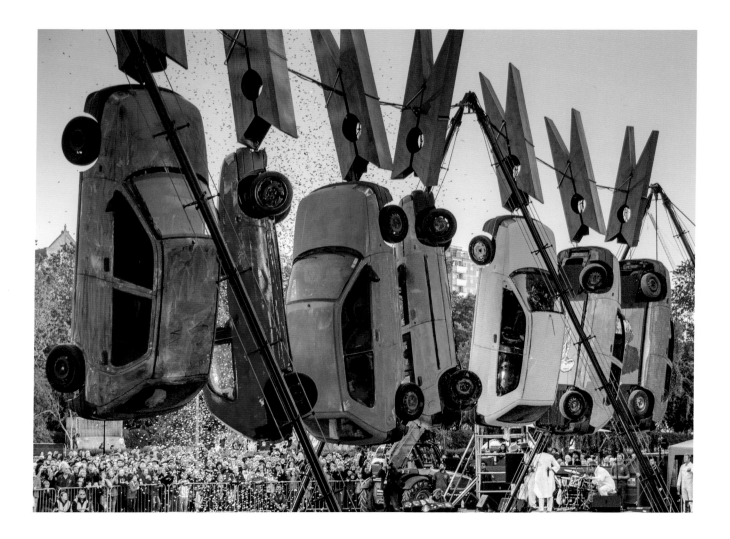

The Birds of St Ann's Well Gardens

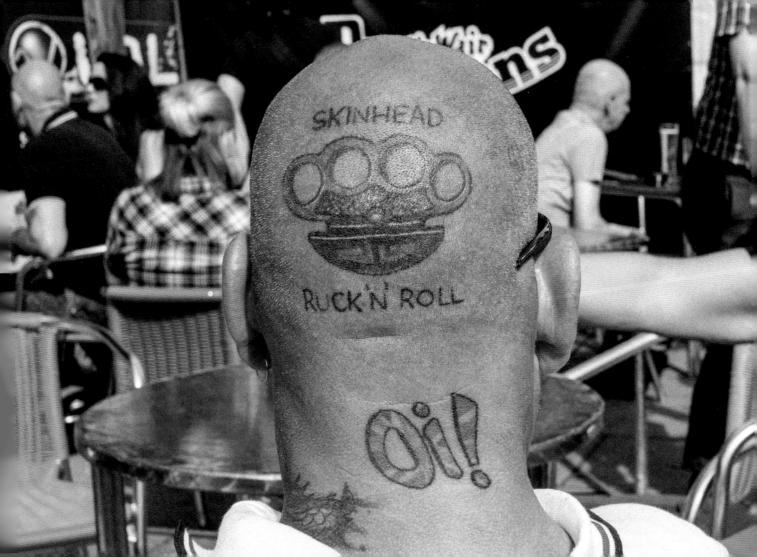

Credits

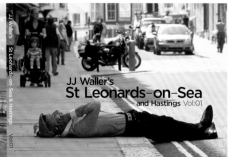

Also available from www.curious-publishing.com
JJ Waller's Brighton Vol 01
JJ Waller's St Leonards-on-Sea and Hastings Vol 01

Dedicated to Eugenie Simmons

With Special Thanks to:
Jasmine Uddin
Mark Power
Nigel Swallow
John Dineen, Waterstones

Design: Transmission
Print: Gemini Brighton

Published by Curious
www.curious-publishing.com

All enquiries and limited edition
print sales: office@jjwaller.com

A catalogue record for this book is available from
the British Library

ISBN 9-780957-439016